The Downfall of American Corrections

Also by Natalie Faulk

Raising Awareness 17 Syllables at a Time: Micropoetry for a Troubled World

Mischief and Nonsense

Raising Awareness Another 17 Syllables at a Time: More Micropoetry for a Troubled World

Whimsy and Mayhem

Levity and Madness

Perpetual Nightmare

Folly and Chaos

Idiocy and Insanity

The Downfall of American Corrections

How Privatization, Mandatory Minimum Sentencing, and the Abandonment of Rehabilitation have Perverted the System beyond Repair

Natalie Faulk

To everyone working in the corrections field who
genuinely seeks and strives toward raising awareness
and changing a severely flawed system, and to the
human beings in U.S. state and federal prisons who
have been harmed by dangerous and flawed
policies and mistreated by overzealous
and unqualified employees.

Preface

The genesis of this book is a result of my nearly three years as an academic instructor for a privately-run New Mexico state prison. My primary function was to provide the necessary knowledge in reading, writing, mathematics, social studies, and science to enable students to successfully pass their general equivalency diploma (GED) test. New Mexico—not unlike other states—mandates that all inmates who do not have a high school diploma or equivalent attend school.

One of the biggest problems with this mandate is the vast number of inmates who have absolutely no desire to attend school or aspiration to obtain a GED frequently risk being written up for noncompliance and/or present a disruption in the classroom. Instead of focusing, first, on those who wish to attend school so they can then take vocational or college courses, prison policies tend to enroll inmates with the least amount of time left, regardless of their academic level or desire. This not only creates problems for those inmates who do not want to be bothered but also among teachers who are left to deal with bad attitudes and needless disruptions.

Whereas I truly loved my job and during my tenure was able to help fourteen of my students obtain their GED certificates, I was painfully aware that many of the four fundamental purposes of criminal punishment—incapacitation, rehabilitation, deterrence, and retribution—were not being effectively realized. Some states, such as New Mexico, for example, are particularly problematic because of the high percentage of state inmates who are housed in private prisons.

The first problem is that prison privatization essentially commoditizes inmates because private companies such as Corrections Corporation of America (CCA) and GEO Group exist to make money. Ergo, they are profit-oriented and in diametrical opposition to the fundamental purpose of corrections. A push for maximum occupancy underlies any efforts at rehabilitation and inmates are commonly given disciplinary reports for truly minor infractions simply to permit the facility to deduct good time, thus ensuring a longer stay.

Additionally—as I witnessed firsthand on a number of occasions—the falsification of said reports and the blatant refusal to adequately investigate instances where the inmate was treated unfairly were abundant. In this type of environment where training is minimal, staff is underpaid, morale is low, and those who have leadership positions are unqualified for such, the inmate is always wrong and the employee is always right, even when the truth proved otherwise. However, when an ethical employee tries to defend a wrongfully accused inmate, he or she is promptly vilified.

Also problematic is the emphasis on making money results in "cutting corners," particularly when it comes to quality and quantity of staff, inmate medical care, quality of food, and rehabilitation programs. When department managers and wardens are enticed by substantial bonuses for saving money, said savings supersede their responsibility to care for and rehabilitate offenders in their care or to ensure staff safety. As many private prisons are constructed in small, out-of-the-way towns, the employment pool is comprised of those who already reside in such towns, many of whom lack the necessary knowledge, skills, and awareness to perform a job with such serious responsibility and expansive magnitude. Little effort is expended into recruiting quality employees, and considerable effort is wasted toward fostering a hostile work environment for the few quality employees they do manage to obtain.

Relatedly, the overemphasis on retribution over rehabilitation is problematic in that by failing to provide inmates with knowledge, job skills, and treatment programs to not reoffend, the revolving door continues and recidivism rates rise. When one realizes that ninety percent of prison inmates will, at some point, be released back into society, it becomes even more critical to ensure they do not reoffend and return to prison but, instead, become law-abiding and productive members of society. Sadly, this is the last thing private prisons desire because rehabilitation reduces populations which, subsequently, diminishes private corporations' profits.

Compounding the problem is the removal of judicial discretion and replacement with an over-emphasis on mandatory minimum sentencing practices that punish the crime and not the offender. Rarely does a one-size-fits-all approach work, and in this respect, it fails miserably. Not only does this practice neglect the offender by oftentimes over-sentencing a first-time, nonviolent offender who would be better served in diversion, treatment, and/or community corrections, but it also fails society as a whole by exposing lower-level offenders to more serious "convicts" who have significant influence. Thus, instead of fixing the problem, current policies simply exacerbate it.

I am fully aware that a large majority of Americans believe that we should simply lock these criminals up and throw away the key. This is an overly simplistic view because it fails to comprehend the effect on society as a whole. They say the true mark of a civilized society is how it treats its elderly and its inmates and, in my opinion, the United States fails miserably at both. While, indeed, there are some individuals who need to be locked up because they are predatory, violent, and/or pure evil, a large percentage of current inmates are simply human beings who have made mistakes just like everyone else in the world. Granted, while some of these mistakes were heinous and deserving of serious punishment, not helping those who want to and can change creates a vicious cycle that undermines and jeopardizes public safety while permitting prison populations to expand.

My question is to what end? Until every person in the United States is incarcerated? Of course, this sounds ridiculous; however, if the current course is maintained with high recidivism rates, the criminalization of other behaviors, and inadequate rehabilitation, then this is not an unbelievable outcome best left for science fiction literature. The current state of corrections is unsustainable—plain and simple. If there are not enough resources to accommodate the current number of inmates in jails, prisons, and on parole and probation then how can any increase be viable?

I have a profound interest in promoting effective rehabilitation processes for our incarcerated population. After all, my entire adult life has been studying, researching, writing about, and working in the criminal justice system in some capacity. However, it was my experience as an academic instructor that really opened my eyes to the necessity for prison reform and the ills of privatization. Not everyone in prison—or jail—is a horribly evil person. It is no secret that many of the most unethical and vile people are walking around free wreaking havoc. As I previously mentioned, the majority of prison inmates are fallible human beings who have made terrible decisions, but should these mistakes—particularly by nonviolent, lower-level offenders—penalize them for life? Are they not worthy of redemption and the opportunity to change their lives by obtaining an education, vocational training, and substance abuse and other mental health treatment?

I hope my words make just one person rethink his or her views on the subject. Any more after that will be a bonus.

Natalie Faulk
4 October 2016

Contents

The Downfall of American Corrections

The Role of Criminal Punishment

Natalie Faulk

Punishing individuals who break the law is society's way of expressing "aggressive antipathy, anger, hatred, or disgust" and to deprive an offender of some ill-begotten advantage as a result of his or her actions.[1] Appropriate punishments are based on whether the sanctions serve the fundamental goals of criminal punishment: offender repentance and recognition of his or her wrongs, behavioral reform, and reconciliation with the victim and society. Further, punishment should be burdensome and painful relative to the actual offense and imposed by an authority or institution whose rules were violated by the offender. Because offenders cannot repay most costs associated with their actions—such as is the case with crimes against persons—other penalties are required to address the wrong.

The philosophy of punishment is controversial due to mixed beliefs over its proper justification and goals and how public perception and attitudes differ from actual practice. Punishment has been largely justified and rationalized under utilitarian and retributive theory in that individuals willingly relinquish some of their rights and submit to governmental authority in exchange for government protection of the rest of their rights. When individuals violate their "contract" with society by breaking the law, such protection is lost and they must be punished.

Contemporary punishment is based on four fundamental goals: incapacitation, retribution, rehabilitation, and deterrence. Whereas each theory has its own rational justification, more often than not they are in conflict with each other. First, incapacitation, quite simply, separates offenders from the rest of society to protect the public and to ensure that the offender does not reoffend. Additionally, incapacitation addresses an offender's dangerousness and assumes incapacitation—via imprisonment—can effectively control future crime.

While this may be the case in the short-term, incapacitation has become less effective because, instead of considering the offender's current offense, greater consideration of an offender's potential future criminality forms the foundation for determining an appropriate punishment. Another problem is that incapacitation works only if those individuals who are incarcerated would have committed additional offenses if left free and do not commit additional offenses after release.[2]

Whereas incapacitation satisfies society's immediate and pressing need to detain and restrain an offender, there is no scientific basis for sentence determination. Because the United States has the highest incarceration rate in the world, questions arise as to its overall effectiveness. Another pressing question is whether the climbing prison populations are actually behind the recent decrease in crime rates or if—as numerous studies suggest—crime itself is decreasing.

Second, retribution seeks to achieve "just deserts;" however, it is criticized and labeled as simple vengeance. Retributive theory is based on Rousseau's (1762) social contract theory—later expounded upon by Hobbes—that places justification for a punishment on the fact that an individual breached his or her end of the contract made with society and, thus, should be punished for his or her actions.

Because its basis is the biblical law of *lex talionis*, or "an eye for an eye," retributive theory holds that any punishment should inflict the same level and type of harm on the offender that the offender inflicted on his or her victim. In other words, the punishment should fit the crime. Despite being confused with vengeance, of particular concern is that whereas limits are placed on retribution by virtue of laws, there are typically no limits for vengeance.

Third, rehabilitation endeavors to identify deviant patterns of behavior and to provide tools for offenders' future success; however, this goal has fallen out of favor due to increased crime rates during the 1980's and 1990's. Rehabilitation assumes that deviance is a social disease and assesses an offender's susceptibility to treatment in order to correct defective behaviors.[3] Thus, rehabilitation attempts to synthesize the offender's background and past behavior with the current offense to determine how to "fix" the problem by changing his or her values, beliefs, morals, and norms to make them more aligned with the majority. In order to accomplish this lofty goal, rehabilitative punishments are uniquely tailored to fit each offender's needs and capacities.

Rehabilitation was the central goal of the American criminal justice system until the last quarter of the twentieth century as evidenced by the adoption of the American Law Institute's Model Penal Code in 1962 that emphasized indeterminate treatment over retribution.[4] Whereas rehabilitation is generally supported by the public for juvenile offenders, support for adults is not as strong, particularly for those with extensive criminal histories.

Of primary concern is that in order for treatment to be effective it must be voluntary. Forcing rehabilitation on offenders who have neither the desire nor ability to change has little chance of success. However, even with an offender's desire to change, the evidence demonstrates that rehabilitative and therapeutic programs, by themselves, are insufficient and must be accompanied by other, more punitive elements.

This roadblock of sorts led to Martinson's (1974) famous article that "nothing works" with respect to offenders and ushered in the demise of rehabilitation as a desired and feasible theory of punishment. As a result, individualized treatment was set aside in favor of the justice model that treats offenders equally based solely on their crimes. Further, rehabilitation proponents were frequently attacked as being soft on crime, thus accounting for its waning public support. This lack of support for rehabilitation continues today.

Finally, deterrence seeks to dissuade future criminal behavior based on the threat of punishment alone. In this capacity, deterrence is simply another word for prevention. Deterrence tries to identify what is most likely to discourage a specific offender—or a group of offenders—from offending, and this model gains the majority of its support from its presumed potential.[5] Essentially, deterrence theory suggests that punishing a few offenders for a particular crime will dissuade others from committing the same offense because of the associated unwanted consequence for doing so.

The Downfall of American Corrections

Of primary importance—and frequently overlooked—is in order to work, potential offenders must know the rules for behavior and then conduct rational cost-benefit analyses prior to acting. The majority of potential offenders fail to do this because they are poor with math or—and more likely—are indifferent to future consequences.[6] This is especially problematic with offenders under the age of twenty-five because of emerging literature that demonstrates the human brain is not fully developed until one's mid-twenties. Further, executive, frontal lobe reasoning, decision-making, impulse control, and appreciating potential long-term outcomes are among the last skills to develop.

With respect to deterrence, there are two types. Specific deterrence is geared toward discouraging a specific individual from reoffending, and if he or she is incarcerated then this goal is automatically fulfilled. Problems with specific deterrence arise when a released offender does, in fact, reoffend. On the other hand, general deterrence posits that other people will be deterred from offending because of the threat of punishment. The literature has demonstrated time and time again that general deterrence does not work, largely because of the lack of certainty, swiftness, and, oftentimes, severity of punishment.

These concepts were at the core of Beccaria's *On Crime and Punishment* (1764) in which the renowned criminologist and father of the Classical school of criminology argued for criminal justice reform—a topic that remains at the forefront of contemporary American jurisprudence. Take capital punishment, for example. The literature is rife with data demonstrating states that continue to utilize the death penalty as a legitimate punishment consistently have higher homicide rates than states without it.

Regardless of which theory is addressed, they all share a common, fundamental goal—to prevent crime and reduce recidivism. Another point of similarity among these concepts is the morality of punishment. Any system that fails to establish legitimacy and credibility risks increasing the stigmatization of offenders, injustice-fueled resistance, and a lack of cooperation among all stakeholders.[7]

Incarceration has become the go-to punishment in the United States, and it is clear that goals have not been fully realized as evidenced by the increasing prison population. Compounding the problem is the subsequent utilization of privately-run prisons which further marginalize inmates by making them simple commodities to be bought and sold; not to mention failing to improve public safety and prevent crime because of private facilities' emphasis on profit. Thus, it makes little sense for private prisons to support any crime reducing policies or punishment reforms whatsoever because improvements in this regard would seriously affect their bottom line.

There is a fifth rationale, however. Restorative justice seeks to blend criminal and civil law and shifts the focus from the offender to repairing the harm done to society. Said repair is accomplished by forcing the offender to take responsibility and accountability for his or her actions, to mend the damage via restitution opportunities, and to make society whole again. Restorative justice understands that punishment in and of itself is insufficient to change behavior and also disrupts the community by warehousing individuals. Instead, this model focuses on problem solving, establishing a dialogue and negotiation between the offender and the victim, and making the community whole.[8]

Restorative justice has demonstrated considerable success in the juvenile justice system, largely due to the fact that juveniles tend to be more amenable to alternatives and are more malleable than adults when it comes to behavioral changes. Despite significant evidence attesting to restorative justice's success, criticism remains, most notably in that victims are given more attention than the offender and that restitution may not be applicable for every crime.[9]

This is not to say that all offenders should be handled within a restorative justice framework. Those who are innately evil and those who are serious, violent, and chronic offenders should, no doubt, be incarcerated, sometimes for life. However, for those offenders who are nonviolent and amenable to treatment, restorative justice seeks to promote offender accountability, victim reparation, offender rehabilitation, and societal restoration with greater potential for success and typically at a lesser cost, both financially and otherwise.

A Brief History of American Corrections

The Beginning

Since the first penitentiaries, American prisons have undergone quite an evolution. At the turn of the twentieth century, the Big House was the most common penal model, and is the direct descendant of earlier penitentiaries. The Big House's fundamental purpose was, simply, to humanely warehouse lawbreakers. Warehousing is the key word here, as there were no daily routines or activities to occupy prisoners' time, nor did these facilities serve any substantive purpose. Prisoners' basic needs were met; however, beyond that there was little activity and few distractions. Further, cells were oftentimes cramped and barren as prisoners' possessions were limited. Food was also rather nondescript and served only to provide calories and energy. Finally, not unlike today, minorities were overrepresented.

During prisons' evolutionary period, three notable changes occurred that signaled a shift from the Big House penitentiary model: introduction of tobacco, abolition of corporal punishment, and emergence of substantial freedoms for prisoners.[10] The first notable change began in the 1940's and extended through the 1950's when, instead of functioning strictly for punishment, prisons became more accommodating and relaxed as evidenced by less intrusive punishment, increased mail and visitation policies, greater recreational activities, and certain amenities such as movies. Additionally, educational, vocational, and therapeutic programs came into being.[11] However, while these types of programs were promised, they were not fully realized, thus resulting in a similar boredom that plagued the earlier Big House.

Absent activities to pass the long and seemingly endless days, frustrations grew, as did violence among inmates. Consequently, racial and ethnic cliques emerged which further contributed to the problems inherent to inmates' lack of direction. Of particular note is that minorities continued to be overrepresented.

The 1970's heralded a push toward improved rehabilitative efforts with experts providing a theoretical framework designed to achieve the greatest results. In order for any rehabilitative program to work it must be designed to target specific problems and characteristics known to be precursors of future criminality, implemented in a manner appropriate for the participating offenders, and delivered as designed by properly experienced and trained staff. Successful programs must also require participants to spend adequate time in the program, utilize cognitive and behavioral treatment methods which are steeped in research and existing best practices, target those offenders at the highest risk for recidivating, and provide considerable positive reinforcement in order to cultivate prosocial behavior. Granted, while these specifics appear to be grounded in common sense, in reality, practice has repeatedly failed to achieve the stated goals.

Following increased crime rates in the 1980's — particularly of violent crimes — the rehabilitative model was gradually usurped by a more retributive mindset. Consequently, contemporary prisons continue to be called correctional institutions despite scant resemblance to past prisons except for physical appearance. During this time, a dichotomy emerged. The retributive push resulted in increasingly longer sentences for offenders, while the punitive sting of punishment was softened by increasing luxuries such as televisions, state-of-the-art fitness equipment, libraries with law sections, commissary privileges where inmates can supplement their daily diet with coffee and other "treats," and various job opportunities, with some occurring outside of the facility, albeit supervised. Thus, even though offenders were given longer sentences, they had these so-called "luxuries" to occupy their daily lives.

Instead of rehabilitating offenders, however, many correctional facilities spend millions of dollars on ensuring that their inmates are occupied but fail to provide the necessary treatment and education required to promote reentry and reintegration back into society. Another common problem—particularly in private facilities—is the lackadaisical attitude by corrections staff to even want to participate in offender rehabilitation. Many facilities are run and staffed by people who desire to do as little amount of work as possible, and this mindset has resulted in myriad reasons to justify a facility lockdown to effectively eschew having to perform their duties. After all, it is much easier to keep inmates locked in their cells or housing pods rather than having to let them out to go to school, work, drug rehabilitation, or any other rehabilitative endeavor. The end result is a population of released inmates who were not given any tools to help them become law-abiding, productive citizens, thus almost ensuring that they will reoffend and return to prison.

Another enduring problem reminiscent of early corrections is the existence of racial and ethnic division and resulting violence. Many scholars assert that "race forms perhaps the key fault line in today's prison community."[12] As a result, prison violence is at an all-time high, spurred largely from chronic overcrowding and lack of effective rehabilitative outlets.

Women's facilities merit mention as well in this discussion. Whereas women's correctional facilities underwent a similar evolution to men's, the most notable difference was that the former resembled dormitories more so than prisons. Additionally, women's facilities' policies were even more liberal; however, there were and continues to be many inmates who are victimized — oftentimes sexually — by male staff. Again, these problems are significantly more rampant in private facilities where the quality of staff is compromised in favor of making a profit.

Goals of American Prisons

The fundamental goal of the American prison system, according to the United States Department of Justice (DOJ) is to "[p]rotect American society by providing for the safe, secure, and humane confinement of persons in federal custody."[13] However, increasingly stringent sentencing guidelines and steadily rising inmate populations over the past several decades have taxed the DOJ's resources. Ongoing budget cuts have resulted in significant deficits to maintain an adequate prison capacity that ensures violent offenders are incarcerated and protects the public. With a steady increase in the inmate population across the country, legislators have looked elsewhere to enable correctional goals to be met.

One of these alternatives is prison privatization, a movement that has gained immense popularity among states which have exceeded their corrections budgets by ongoing new facility construction. Perhaps the biggest problem with this rapid growth is that corrections budgets continue to swell, thus creating an even greater financial deficit and leading many reformers to examine more community-based and cost-effective options.

Natalie Faulk

Community-based corrections proponents like
myself assert that ongoing warehousing of
offenders—especially lower-level, nonviolent ones—
increases association with violent and so-called career
criminals, thus potentially cultivating nonviolent
offenders' propensity to reoffend upon release. Rising
prison populations among decreasing funds creates
huge deficits in educational, vocational, treatment,
and other rehabilitative programs necessary to ensure
that released inmates are able to successfully reenter
and reintegrate back into society. Diverting critical
resources in this direction—instead of continuing to
construct new prisons—will provide greater long
term benefits and cost savings than the endless cycle
of building prisons and hiring guards.

Prison Populations

According to the Prison Policy Initiative, the United States currently has 2.3 million people incarcerated in some form; this represents more people per capita than any other industrialized nation in the world. Every year, nearly 640,000 people are released from prison while individuals go to jail a whopping eleven million times per year.[14] Granted, the majority of those entering jail make bail or are released on their own recognizance while a relatively small number are actually sentenced. Of those individuals who are convicted and sentenced, as many as one-in-five are incarcerated for a nonviolent drug offense, and this figure does not include those who have plea bargained to a different offense or those whose more serious crime essentially trumped the additional but lesser included drug offense. Additionally, there are almost 820,000 individuals currently on parole and 3.8 million on probation.[15]

Of the thirty-three thousand incarcerated juveniles in the United States, just over seven thousand of them are incarcerated for "offenses" which are not even crimes, such as probation technical violations and status offenses.[16] Status offenses are acts that are not considered to be crimes for adults such as truancy, curfew violations, underage drinking, running away, and incorrigibility; however, for juveniles, these actions constitute deviant behaviors which subject them to arrest, adjudication, and punishment.

Finally, another forty-two thousand people are incarcerated for criminal violations of United States immigration laws or are civilly detained by the United States Immigration and Customs Enforcement (ICE). These populations are simply unsustainable, and locking more people up or relying more heavily on private prisons is not the answer. Policymakers must take an honest look at the actual issues and make objective, rational, and humane decisions to rectify a serious problem.

Racial and Ethnic Inequalities

It is quite obvious that the American criminal justice system—particularly corrections—has significant racial implications. Despite comprising approximately thirty percent of the United States' population, Blacks and Hispanics comprise fifty-six percent of the incarcerated population.[17] In fact, the evidence demonstrates that one in three adult Black males will be arrested at some point in their lives; compared to one in six Hispanic males and one in seventeen White males.[18]

The prevailing view is that Blacks commit a disproportionate amount of crimes and, as would be expected, this assertion has raised considerable debate amidst a growing body of evidence demonstrating that there are, in fact, dramatic differences among races with respect to crime rates. According to Rubenstein (2016), Blacks have notably higher crime rates in several categories and across all age groups, especially for violent crimes. In fact, in 2013, a Black male was six times more likely to commit murder than a non-Black, and twelve times more likely to murder someone of another race than to actually be murdered by someone of another race.[19] Of the approximately 660,000 interracial crimes between Blacks and Whites in 2013, Blacks were the perpetrators eighty-five percent of the time.[20]

In some of the United States' most dangerous cities, the disparity is enormous. For example, Rubenstein (2016) reports that if New York City was all White, the murder rate would drop by ninety-one percent, robbery by eighty-one percent, and shootings in general by ninety-seven percent.[21] If the same held true for Chicago, Illinois, the homicide rate would decrease by ninety percent, rape by eighty-one percent, and robbery by ninety percent.[22]

Even if Blacks do, indeed, commit a greater proportion of violent crimes relative to their concentration in the general population, other factors contribute to the vast overrepresentation of Blacks in American prisons. Among these factors include an increased likelihood of Black—as well as Hispanic—individuals being searched by police, arrested, and treated more harshly from the initial charging through sentencing. Compounding the problem is chronic underfunding of states' public defenders' offices and so-called "race neutral" criminal justice policies which are anything but.

As mentioned, the evidence suggests that Black and Hispanic people are overrepresented in prisons and jails because they commit a larger proportion of the crime; however, this fails to account for additional obstacles such as the ongoing socioeconomic disadvantage plaguing many "minority" communities. Thus, this geographically concentrated, socioeconomic disadvantage naturally results in higher rates of certain violent and property crimes.[23] Ghandnoosh (2015) identifies four primary sources perpetuating racism in the criminal justice system: the aforementioned ostensibly race neutral policies and laws, systemic prejudice in the criminal justice system, resource allocation policies and decisions that disadvantage those of lower socioeconomic status, and criminal justice policies that exacerbate preexisting socioeconomic problems.

The Downfall of American Corrections

One of the most heinous examples of alleged race-neutral policies is the powder cocaine versus crack cocaine disparity that prescribed similar penalties for a substantially larger amount of powder cocaine than crack cocaine. Of particular importance was that minorities in inner cities overwhelmingly used crack. While the Fair Sentencing Act of 2010 reduced the disparity between the two from 100:1 to 18:1—with some states like California eliminating this disparity completely—the Smarter Sentencing Act of 2015, if passed, will enable retroactive reduction of mandatory minimum sentences for certain drug offenses. Other efforts to address racially disparate policies include halting the prosecution of minor marijuana possession, conducting racial impact studies prior to enacting legislation, and reexamining risk assessment instruments for bias.

With respect to prejudice, the literature is rife with studies that have identified implicit racial bias among police officers, prosecutors, judges, jurors, probation and parole officers, and even defense attorneys who—along with probation and parole officers—are oftentimes burdened with unsustainable caseloads due to the failure of policymakers and other officials to allocate adequate funds and manpower. The issue of police officer prejudice has been quite prevalent following a spate of police officer involved shootings — as both shooters and victims — within the national spotlight.

These shootings have been at the core of increasing attention on and scrutiny of the use of excessive force by police. Does this happen? Yes, sadly. Does it occur as much as the mainstream media and liberal politicians allege? No. In fact, most violent crime is intra-racial. The Bureau of Justice Statistics (BJS), National Crime Victimization Survey (NCVS) reported that between 2012 and 2013, Whites were victimized fifty-six percent of the time by other Whites; Blacks were victimized just over sixty-two percent of the time by other Blacks, and Hispanics were victimized nearly thirty-nine percent of the time by other Hispanics — each accounting for the largest rate of victimization within each racial and ethnic group.

It is important to discuss the issue of police officers fatally shooting Black men as it has been pervasive in the media during this presidential election year, with varying narratives put forth to demonstrate why "we" are right and "they" are wrong. According to Mac Donald (2016), in 2015, police officers killed six hundred and sixty-two Whites and Hispanics, for fifty percent of all fatal police shootings, and two hundred and fifty-eight Blacks, for twenty-six percent of all fatal police shootings. Contrary to popular belief, the evidence demonstrates the vast majority of these victims were "armed or otherwise threatening the officer with potentially lethal force."[24]

Of course, some may allege such statistics are evidence of racism among police officers since Whites comprise sixty-two percent of the population while Blacks comprise just thirteen percent; however, the BJS reported that in 2009, Blacks were charged with sixty-percent of all robberies, fifty-seven percent of all homicides, and forty-five percent of all assaults.[25] Thus, Mac Donald asserts, the twenty-six percent Black homicide rate by police should actually be larger given the much higher crime rate and the fact that most police use of force incidents occur when officers interact with violent offenders.

Furthermore, a special prosecutor hired by the DOJ found that Black and Hispanic police officers are more likely to fire at Blacks than are White officers— at the rate of 3.3 times higher. Finally, Mac Donald identified FBI data demonstrating that forty percent of cop killers are Black; thus making officers 18.5 times more likely to be killed by a Black person than a police officer killing an unarmed Black person.[26] So, while, yes, there is evidence of racism among police agencies, the incidence is considerably lower than some believe. Quite simply, there is no epidemic of White police officers shooting unarmed Black citizens.

Nevertheless, in response to the increasing scrutiny of law enforcement officers, many police departments have reexamined their use of force policies and some states such as Connecticut, Maryland, and Wisconsin have employed special prosecutors to handle unlawful use of force complaints to eliminate the potential conflict of interests when jurisdictional prosecutors bring cases against officers.

Departments have also been increasing recruitment efforts toward Blacks and Hispanics in order to improve community policing and the building of cooperative relationships between police and the communities they serve. Technological innovations such as body cameras have also been introduced to make law enforcement more transparent and, thus, more accountable. While these efforts have the potential to improve community relations and protect both police officers' and citizens' safety, the ongoing skewed narratives perpetrated by politicians and others in the public eye who are using media overrepresentation of police use of force cases make improvement difficult and reduce the likelihood that the general population will buy into any legitimate efforts to address these issues.

As for inadequate resource allocation policies that disadvantage lower-income people, bail is perhaps the biggest concern. With over sixty percent of pretrial detainees unable to post bail, the longer arrestees wait in jail the higher the likelihood they will be convicted, accept unfavorable plea bargains, and, ultimately, be sent to prison.[27] Underfunded community corrections options and treatment programs also disadvantage lower-income defendants by providing substandard care and failing to address offenders' specific needs. Finally, and perhaps most egregious, probation and parole conditions that require probationers and parolees to obtain a job, attend treatment, and report at certain times and places—oftentimes having to rely on public transportation—lead to increased problems for these individuals lacking the basic resources to do so. Whereas each single incident of racial bias may not appear to be significant, the cumulative effect is.[28] Compounding the problem is that not only are those who have served time affected by current criminal justice policies, but their families and neighborhoods are as well, further perpetuating a vicious cycle that disproportionately affects minority communities.

The fact remains, without a doubt, that the criminal justice system perpetuates racism and requires overhaul; however, pointing fingers and playing the blame game without being fully armed with the facts results in what the United States is currently experiencing: a rise in politically motivated activist movements that are pushing an unfounded narrative to further their own outlandish goals while being supported by liberal, "progressive" politicians and wealthy celebrities who whine and cry about oppression and discrimination or suggest ridiculous and more divisive "solutions" without actually doing anything about the issues themselves. Solving the problem requires an honest dialogue where everyone contributes to finding a workable solution to benefit all.

Female Inmates

There has also been a significant increase in female inmates as a result of mandatory minimum sentencing guidelines, especially for drug-related offenses. In fact, these two factors have been cited as the primary reasons behind the growing female inmate population which, according to the BLS, is at an all-time high. Specifically, since 1990, the number of female inmates has grown significantly faster than the number of male inmates. For example, between 1977 and 2007, the number of female prisoners increased by an incredible eight hundred and thirty-two percent.[29]

One of the greatest concerns in the female inmate conversation is the high rate of incarcerated mothers and how to effectively weigh punishment against the necessary mother-child bond and long-term recidivism reduction. Since nearly sixty-five percent of all female federal inmates and forty-five percent of state inmates have minor children at the time of their imprisonment, better alternatives are sorely needed.[30]

Compounding the problem is that nearly two-thirds of these women do not even have a high school education, not to mention the high rates of substance abuse problems, mental illness, and a history of physical, emotional, and/or sexual abuse in this population. These issues are more salient for females who are subsequently released because as former inmates, they lose many critical benefits from assistance programs necessary for effective societal reintegration and survival.

An oft-underappreciated outgrowth of the rise in female inmates is the numerous problems faced by children of incarcerated mothers. To address this, some states have revisited the nursery concept so children born to incarcerated women can remain in their mother's care within a correctional facility for a finite amount of time to promote a strong mother-child bond. Such efforts have been repeatedly praised as protecting the child's future success. Whereas these types of programs operate more frequently at the community level such as in residential treatment programs, understandably, there continues to be hesitation regarding implementing them in the prison setting.

Unfortunately, not unlike the aforementioned problems for male inmates, lack of education and access to resources tend to offset any progress made in prison. The natural consequence is higher recidivism rates. Compounding the problem is that incarcerated women who have little or no regular visitation with their children while they are incarcerated are six times more apt to reoffend within their first year post-release.[31] Consequently, experts assert that programs that increase education, address substance abuse, promote better visitation efforts, and provide considerable post-release assistance have the best chance to achieve positive results. Further, because a large proportion of incarcerated mothers have multiple children—oftentimes with multiple partners—efforts to unify families are also critical.

Conclusion

There is a growing consensus that current American incarceration policies are ineffective with respect to crime control and, additionally, are "costly and counterproductive."[32] The United States' habit of locking up people who do not require long term incarceration—petty offenders, nuisances, and the mentally ill—has strained the system beyond its intended purpose, thus giving the United States the dubious distinction of being the nation with the highest incarceration rates. The end result is a criminal justice system that simply adopts inadequate policies that do nothing to reduce crime rates instead of taking an honest look at the actual problems—lack of education, unemployment, poverty, and systemic racism—and expending efforts and resources toward fixing those issues.

Natalie Faulk

Prison Privatization

Background

In July 2010, three inmates escaped from a private medium-security prison in Arizona run by Management and Training Company (MTC). Whereas two of the escapees were quickly apprehended, the third avoided capture for three weeks during which time he murdered an Oklahoma couple in New Mexico.[33] Sadly, stories like this are not uncommon in the privatization discussion.

A post-incident investigation revealed numerous glaring security oversights such as a "faulty perimeter alarm, inadequate maintenance on the alarm system, no security guards posted at the perimeter when the escape occurred, a sluggish response to the reported escape, and nonoperational flood lights at the perimeter."[34] This incident—along with other recent and highly-publicized ones—underscores the myriad problems inherent to the privatization movement and begs the question of whether it is appropriate for governments to delegate important criminal justice functions to the private sector that is, quite simply, ill-equipped for such responsibility.

Private prisons can be defined in myriad ways. Miller (2010) describes privatization as "a transfer of public facilities to a private organization; a contract to design and operate new prisons; and a contract to provide other services to public prisons such as transportation, medical care, food, and maintenance."[35] To accomplish this, private companies enter into a contract with the government to provide specific correctional services in exchange for government oversight in said facilities' regulation; however, the government does not provide direct facility oversight, and this blurs the tenuous line between the two.

Between 1999 and 2010, the number of inmates housed in private prisons increased by eighty percent, while the overall prison population only increased by eighteen percent, thus demonstrating the increasing reliance on private prisons by both state and federal governments.[36] The two largest private prison companies in the United States—CCA and GEO Group—are responsible for over ninety percent of private facilities in the country.

Whereas only seven thousand prisoners were housed in private prisons in 1990, by June 2010, nearly 129,000 of the 1.6 million federal and state inmates in the United States were held in private facilities, thus representing eight percent of the total.[37] Between 1980 and 2013, the number of federal inmates housed in private prisons increased by almost eight hundred percent—accounting for fifteen percent of its total prison population, or almost thirty thousand inmates.[38] While the number of state inmates held in private prisons during that same period grew by a comparably low forty percent, today some states house more than one quarter of their inmates in private prisons.[39] Among those states most reliant on private facilities is New Mexico that boasts over forty percent of its state inmates being held in private facilities.[40]

During this increase between 1980 and 2013, six states—Alabama, Connecticut, Ohio, Pennsylvania, South Carolina, and Vermont—began using private prisons while nine states—Arkansas, Kansas, Maine, Michigan, Minnesota, Nevada, North Dakota, Utah, and Washington eliminated their use of private prisons.[41] Some states reduced their reliance on private facilities such as Wisconsin that cut its number of private prisoners from 3,421 to twenty-five.[42] Finally, some states—Delaware, Illinois, Iowa, Massachusetts, Missouri, Nebraska, New Hampshire, New York, Oregon, Rhode Island, and West Virginia—did not use any private prisons whatsoever.[43]

With respect to Washington, instead of incarcerating many of its own prisoners within the state, officials simply contracted with GEO Group to house them in Michigan. In fact, Baldwin, Michigan's

North Lake Correctional Facility was recently reopened and given a contract with GEO Group. North Lake Correctional Facility was originally opened in 1998 to hold juveniles who were tried and sentenced as adults, but it was closed in 2005 following an audit that identified numerous safety concerns for both inmates and staff. The prison reopened for a short time in 2011 and has since reopened yet again; currently housing prisoners from Washington and Vermont. Of significant concern is that Michigan lawmakers are entertaining the notion of using the oft-troubled prison to house maximum security inmates.

Compounding the problem is that shipping inmates out of state is harmful and poor policy since family members typically cannot afford to travel to visit their loved ones. Part of successful reentry and reintegration is fostering positive, prosocial skills; however, by eliminating visits by family members — particularly children — an important aspect of this positivity is destroyed. Regardless, GEO Group is very happy to renew and extend contracts with states to ship their inmates to GEO facilities because of the potentially high revenues the private company can charge for its services.

Fiscal pressure and politics have played — and continues to play — a significant role in corrections and has been the impetus for the rise in privatization. The widely held assumption is that privatization may reduce certain costs. States and the federal government have used the privatization boon to assert their own economic and political stances.

This larger role has led to increasingly vengeful and punitive criminal justice policies in which more and more behaviors are criminalized, sentences are harsher, and many rehabilitative programs to improve reentry and reintegration have been eliminated. Legislative measures such as the Sentencing Reform Act of 1984, the Violent Crime Control and Law Enforcement Act of 1994, and the Illegal Immigration and Immigrant Responsibility Act of 1996 have all played a significant role in increasing punitive sentencing policies and ensuring private prisons' longevity.[44]

Also to blame is the Washington, D.C. conservative political organization American Legislative Executive Counsel (ALEC) that has historically promoted tough criminal justice legislation thanks to considerable financial contributions to legislators to help promote its and its supporters' political agendas.[45] Unsurprisingly, ALEC also spearheaded support for prison privatization; however, at the heart of the problem is that private prisons blur the necessary lines between politics and business as well as between the public and private sectors.

Politics are influenced greatly by public opinion and fear which have, over the past thirty years, contributed to the failed War on Drugs, rising public fear about crime, and mandatory minimum sentences—each of which has contributed to the ridiculously high incarceration rate in the United States today. Thankfully, there are some states that have the political wherewithal to use common sense and reduce sentencing policies to alleviate budgetary crises and, as a surprising and unexpected side effect, have also enjoyed substantial declines in both crime and incarceration rates.[46] In fact, as of 2003, twenty-five states had enacted sentencing reform legislation while taking other proactive steps in correctional policy and, as a result, were met with considerable success.[47]

Whereas the rational person understands that reducing prison populations and developing better policies and programs to address crime control in this county should occur, those with the power to actually effect change do not share this view. Instead, legislators continue to beat their proverbial heads against the wall by funding programs that have been repeatedly shown to be ineffective and, in many cases, dangerous without any semblance of rationality or logic.

Thus, the rampant growth of private prisons has raised many policy, economic, and constitutional questions as to their effectiveness and legitimacy in contemporary corrections practice. The literature is rife with studies detailing the alleged efficacy of privatization as well as the benefits such facilities supposedly bestow; however, these studies have been oft-criticized due to methodological flaws or researcher bias to promote individual agendas. Of particular concern are constitutional inquiries regarding whether it is proper for states to outsource their responsibility for criminal punishment. At the heart of the debate are salient questions regarding economic viability, labor, safety, security, accountability, transparency, and constitutionality, and whether private facilities fulfill the fundamental goals of criminal punishment.

Natalie Faulk

The Evolution of Private Prisons

The earliest examples of prison privatization date back to the United States' inception. Until 1790, local governments would reimburse private jailers for holding defendants awaiting trial as well as incarcerating individuals who owed debts until such obligations were paid in full. This relationship changed in 1790 with the creation of the first publicly-run prison. The next several decades saw private business playing a greater role in state-run prisons by providing contracted services such as transportation, food preparation, and medical care.[48]

The roots of the contemporary privatization movement can be traced to the convict lease system of the 1880's. Created by private correctional facilities, this system leased prisoners to certain industries—such as construction and the railroad—to work. States received a percentage of the prisoners' income, and, thus, were able to generate a profit. However, due to brutal living conditions, poor hygiene, high mortality rates, malnutrition, overcrowding, discrimination, exploitation, and widespread physical altercations among inmates and guards, this system was eventually deemed unconstitutional.[49]

Subsequent fledgling attempts at modern privatization occurred during the 1970's in the juvenile justice system with the passage of the Juvenile and Delinquency Prevention Act that originally sought to create effective programs to prevent delinquency and to divert juveniles from the traditional system to one where they would receive critically necessary alternatives to incarceration.[50] In reality, however, the Act created substantial incentives for private entities to gain a foothold in the corrections field and, by the mid-1980's, a number of public-private contracts were entered into with respect to adult correctional facilities. The subsequent War on Drugs, adoption of mandatory sentencing policies, deterioration of public prisons, and resulting chronic overcrowding further taxed governments' limited resources, thus paving a yellow brick road toward privatization.

In 1979, Public Law 96-157 created the Private Sector/Prison Industry Enhancement Program (PIE-Program) that permitted states to sell prison-made goods for profit across state lines as long as the inmates were paid a comparable wage. The program taught inmates valuable vocational skills and some of the profit was used to compensate crime victims.[51] The PIE-Program was instrumental in the privatization movement. With increasingly punitive public policies adopted in the 1970's and 1980's due to the War on Drugs and the subsequent embrace of mandatory minimum sentencing, a rapidly rising prison population opened the door for privatization to make a strong reemergence.

Emergence of Correctional Corporation of America and GEO Group

CCA was established in 1983 in response to rapid prison population growth. Claiming a superior capacity to construct and operate federal and state prisons with comparable service at a lower price, its first contract was in Hamilton County, Tennessee. Just two years later, the company sought to assume management of the state's entire prison population; however, significant opposition regarding cost overruns and inmate escapes forced the legislature to nix those plans. Despite this, CCA was awarded additional contracts in Texas, Florida, and Kentucky—as well as others in Tennessee—thus setting the stage for rapid, expansive growth on private prisons.

Wackenhut Corrections Corporation (WCC) began in 1984 and, in 2003, changed its name to GEO Group. Today, CCA and GEO Group oversee the vast majority of private prisons in the United States with combined revenues of over three billion dollars per year.[52] Other private companies with multiple prison contracts across the United States include MTC, LCS Correctional Services, and Emerald Corrections.

Whereas in 1984, only three states embraced the privatization crusade, by 1994, thirty states had done so.[53] Since then, the privatization movement has exploded—particularly since 2011—with a strengthened push for expanding private prisons at the state level. The reasons behind the privatization boom are the explosive growth of incarceration rates courtesy of the failed War on Drugs, mandatory minimum sentencing, the de-emphasis on probation and parole, increasingly punitive "three strikes" laws, reduction of diversion, deteriorating public prison conditions and chronic overcrowding, and the inability of the public sector to effectively address all of these factors.[54]

Of particular concern is the widespread unilateral acceptance of the privatization movement without questioning—or even noticing—ongoing failures within private prisons. As the cliché goes, money talks, and state officials have increasingly accepted substantial campaign contributions from the private prison lobby as they continue to facilitate widespread expansion of private facilities. In fact, between 2003 and 2011, CCA contributed nearly $190,000 per year to state legislators and political action committees to further its cause. CCA spent another $150,000 during this same time to promote or defeat certain ballot initiatives that would be "bad for business."[55] Among referenda private corporations support include "proposals to implement harsher criminal penalties, making prosecutions easier, and eliminating bail for illegal immigrants charged with violent or gang-related felonies."[56] Thus, those promoting privatization are actively lobbying to ensure harsher laws are passed without any regard for how this will further impact the correctional system.

With the underlying motive of private prisons to increase profits and satisfy shareholders—instead of rehabilitating offenders—there is a natural disincentive to fulfill the very goals of corrections. Ensuring that private prisons flourish despite operating in a manner diametrically opposite to contemporary correctional philosophy is, quite simply, bad policy. Mandatory minimum sentences, the failed War on Drugs, "three strikes laws," and a de-emphasis on probation and parole continue to promote a system that essentially encourages recidivism because there is really no other option for many released inmates who were not adequately prepared to become law-abiding and productive members of society.

Recidivism is what private facilities count on. With higher rates of reoffending, more inmates fill more beds and more money goes into private prison administrators' pockets. Further, some states' private prisons enjoy the added benefit of contracts that guarantee them a certain level of occupancy. In fact, Smith (2016) reported that four years ago, CCA's Chief Corrections Officer Harley Lappin—who, incidentally, was the United States Bureau of Prison's (BOP) former director—offered states a "deal" in which CCA would purchase state prisons "in exchange for twenty-year contracts and guaranteed ninety-per-cent occupancy."[57] Private watchdog organization In the Public Interest found, in 2013, that nearly two-thirds of private prison contracts included occupancy guarantees as well as stipulations placing the burden of responsibility for empty beds on taxpayers; undoubtedly without their knowledge.[58]

Essentially, private prisons fail on many levels to adequately deter and rehabilitate offenders because their very existence relies on continued high incarceration rates. Compounding the problem is the profit seeking nature of private facilities leads to cutting corners and the subsequent dangers such deficiencies pose to staff, inmates, and the public. Private prisons have, basically, removed the word "correct" out of corrections entirely.

Arguments for Privatization

Privatization proponents assert that private facilities provide increased "innovation, quality, accountability, access to expertise, efficiency, and flexibility" because of fewer bureaucratic constraints than are present in the public sector.[59] Proponents also claim that ensuring specific contractual provisions that clearly delineate policies and procedures for addressing disciplinary infractions and providing private prisons with state oversight will protect against potential problems; however, the evidence demonstrates that such safeguards have done little to protect the public—and correctional inmates and staff—from a rapidly growing and increasingly troubled inmate population. Finally, proponents emphasize that private prisons can generate significant cost savings; however, the data also demonstrate that supporting studies are methodologically flawed and there is very little if any savings over state-run facilities.

This final point—that private prisons can provide greater cost savings—has been at the center of the privatization debate since its inception. Ample estimations exist purporting that private facilities cost twenty to thirty percent less than public prisons;

however, such cost comparisons are rife with methodological issues as to how, exactly, these costs are calculated. A number of indirect costs related to legal contracts, monitoring, and financial liability cannot easily be included into a cost-benefit analysis.[60] Further, per the economy of scale theory, facilities with a higher inmate population generally have lower per diem costs, thus negating the utility of cross comparisons. Additionally, questions arise as to the type and location of facilities, number and type of inmates, available programs, and facility size; each of which has the potential to skew results and offer misleading conclusions. Finally, there is no way to prove whether private facilities' alleged cost savings are, indeed, accurate because of the tendency to misrepresent certain costs and other factors to demonstrate adherence to state and American Correctional Association (ACA) guidelines.

Natalie Faulk

Arguments against Privatization

Conversely, opponents have questioned from the beginning whether inmates will receive adequate supervision and care, and, again, the data demonstrate that such fears are, indeed, warranted. There is mounting evidence that not only do private prisons fail to protect the public but they also fail to provide adequate safety and rehabilitation to offenders in myriad ways. Among the most cited reasons include untrained and undisciplined staff, poorly designed and constructed facilities, low employee compensation with few benefits, high staff turnover rates, failure to effectively address inmate misconduct, and a lack of real oversight by state authorities.[61]

Labor

Labor is one of the most discussed budgetary concerns in the privatization debate. Private facilities, in their efforts to cut costs and maximize their profits, tend to have very high ratios of prisoners to guards, with some facilities having a mere five correctional officers on duty to oversee as many as seven hundred and fifty inmates.[62] Whereas a vast majority of states spend as much as ninety-six percent of their prison budgets on salaries, benefits, supplies, maintenance, and other contractual services, private prisons are loath to commit such serious expenditures because of the potential profit decreases. For example, in 2005 alone, state correctional officers earned nearly $280 million in overtime pay due to understaffing stemming from chronic overcrowding.[63] Private facilities would never expend this much because of the associated profit reductions. Instead, private facilities repeatedly operate with inadequate staff, thus decreasing safety not only for employees but for inmates and the public should inmates escape.

Private prison employees earn significantly lower wages, receive inadequate training, and are largely inexperienced. As a result, private facilities experience ridiculously high turnover rates. Yet, these facilities continue to get away with this disparity because of the absence of union protection in the private sector. Granted, unionization is not a labor panacea because there is ample literature demonstrating negative aspects of unions; however, in this case, unionization would not only protect employees who work in a very dangerous field but would also ensure that the fundamental goals of the criminal justice system are upheld without having to worry about such efforts decreasing potential profit.

Consequently, lower pay often results in a decrease in staff morale, thus resulting in weaker controls and an increase in inmate-on-inmate and inmate-on-staff assaults. Several reports have suggested such assaults are at least fifty percent higher in private prisons than public ones.[64]

Safety

The aforementioned problems of unqualified and underqualified prison guards in private facilities are directly to blame for increased physical altercations between inmates and between inmates and staff. For example, between September 2007 and September 2008, the CCA-run Idaho Correctional Center reported one hundred and thirty-two inmate-on-inmate assaults, compared to only forty-two similar assaults at the state-run Idaho State Correctional Institution during that same period. At the time, each facility housed approximately fifteen hundred inmates.[65]

Safety concerns are not simply limited to staff and the general public. Among the most recent reports wherein inmates were harmed include allegations of brutality at the GEO Group-run Walnut Grove Youth Correctional Facility in Mississippi; accusations against a prison psychiatrist at a CCA-run facility in Florida for sexual abuse of female inmates including requests for lap dances and offers to trade drugs in exchange for sex; 2010 footage showing how guards at CCA's Idaho Correctional Center stood around as inmates beat each other into comas; and a 2007 incident at the CCA-run Elizabeth Detention Center in New Jersey in which an African male inmate was left alone for thirteen hours after sustaining a head injury from which he died, during which time officials discussed whether to send his body back to Guinea to detract attention from the death.[66]

Substandard medical care has also caused significant inmate injury. From CCA facilities' refusing to fill prisoners' legitimate prescriptions and failures by medical staff to demonstrate sufficient health training to GEO Group prisons downgrading mental health diagnoses and discontinuing necessary medications or not providing mental health care when requested, it is tragically obvious that making money trumps these private corporations' capacity to provide proper care to individuals who they are supposed to house humanely and rehabilitate.[67]

In another example, a 2013 lawsuit by twenty-five inmates alleged that a physician who worked at two New Mexico GEO facilities—Northeast New Mexico Detention Facility in Clayton and Guadalupe County Correctional Facility in Santa Rosa—sexually abused his inmate patients. The lawsuit also stated that this physician failed to wear gloves while examining inmates, thus forsaking hygiene and proper disease prevention, and that the facilities failed to ensure the integrity of examinations by not having a third person present. Despite repeated reports by inmates about the abuse—and observations by other staff—prison administrators failed to do anything, and the plaintiffs eventually won their lawsuit against GEO and the facilities.

Ultimately, the costs of poor quality supervision and other negligence are transferred to a public that has to deal with escapees, increased medical expenses due to rising altercations, and higher legal costs as a result of prison lawsuits. For example, in March 2012, the New Mexico Department of Corrections levied almost $1.1 million in penalties and fines against GEO Group for inadequate staffing at GEO's Lea County Correctional Facility in Hobbs as well as nearly $11,800 in fines against CCA for failure to adequately staff its women's prison in Grants.[68] Despite GEO Group's agreement to spend $200,000 over the next several years to recruit additional employees at the three New Mexico prisons it oversees—in Hobbs, Santa Rosa, and Clayton—said facilities continue to be understaffed, not only with respect to correctional officers but also noncustodial positions such as mental health providers, substance abuse counselors, and academic and vocational instructors, and many of these positions have remained, and continue to remain, vacant for over sixty days, in violation of state ACA standards.

Another result of inadequate staffing is the failure of private facilities to release inmates on time. Part of CCA's aforementioned penalty stemmed from its failure to release fifteen inmates on time, with thirteen of them being released more than a month past their release dates.[69] New Mexico is not the only state where fines and penalties are ubiquitous. A successful wrongful death lawsuit against a GEO Group facility in Oklahoma resulted in a $6.5 million damage award to survivors of an inmate who was beaten to death by his cellmate.[70]

Even more troubling are additional, less publicized yet egregious violations. Returning again to New Mexico, it was only after current Governor Susana Martinez took office that CCA and GEO Group began to worry about contractual obligation violations and subsequent penalties. Despite the existence of state employed contract monitors in each private facility, these monitors have no enforcement authority and, thus, private facilities are basically free to violate state mandates without any punishment. The severity of such issues came to light in 2010 when the state's Legislative Finance Committee examined then-Governor Bill Richardson's administration and determined that the state had failed to impose nearly $18.6 million in fines for inadequate staffing in private facilities.[71] Many believe that this is only the tip of a much larger iceberg and serves as a clear warning regarding the lack of accountability, transparency, and legitimacy endemic among private prisons.

Constitutionality

Another criticism of privatization is whether the state has the right to delegate certain governmental powers to a non-governmental agency since society's right to punish wrongdoers is derived from the citizens themselves.[72] Because of the shift of control, private prison inmates are not protected under the equal protection clause of the Fifth and Fourteenth Amendments, further undermining the government's constitutional commitment to the law and, essentially, perpetuating a form of neo-slavery. In the end, the increased use of private prisons undermines governments' efforts and commitment to preserving the law and maintaining social accountability as inmates are relegated to little more than property to be bought and sold.

Additionally, chronically overcrowded prisons violate inmates' Eighth Amendment protection against cruel and unusual punishment, and this ongoing problem has led to a number of state courts and United States Supreme Court decisions in which judges ordered states to alleviate their chronically overcrowded prisons to reduce constitutional liability. A striking example is California's 2011 Public Safety Realignment Initiative (AB 109 and 117) that forced state prisons to reduce their population; however, the state "solved" this problem by transferring—and subsequently sentencing non-serious, non-sexual, and nonviolent offenders—to county jails. As would be expected, this effort simply shifted the burden to the jails which have also fallen prey to chronic overcrowding.

Costs

Perhaps the most cited argument in the entire privatization dialogue is whether private prisons do, in fact, reduce costs borne by states. Accusations levied against lawmakers for "willfully fund[ing] the front end of tough on crime bills without considering the budgetary concerns caused by new prisoners and the new prisons needed to house them" suggest that the answer is a resounding no.[73] Relatedly, many opponents assert that private facilities are only cost-effective in the short term because the growing need for maintaining a rapidly rising prison population will result in staggering long-term costs.

Of primary concern is since private facilities' primary goal is profit, they simply do not care enough to perform the job they were contracted to do, as evidenced by the growing rate of assaults, corruption, and escapes. This provides even more compelling evidence supporting the growing assertion that private companies seemingly do not care about inmate rehabilitation or public safety. The profit margin for private prisons is staggering. In 2010, CCA enjoyed profits of nearly $1.7 billion, while GEO Group's profits were only slightly less at $1.6 billion.[74]

Also problematic is that CCA and GEO Group administer over seventy-five percent of private prisons.[75] As of June 2012, CCA owned and operated ninety-one thousand beds in sixty-six facilities in twenty states and Washington, D.C, while GEO Group owned and operated 65,716 beds in sixty-six facilities.[76] Very little of the corporations' profits are directed into the facilities they oversee to ensure proper security, safety, staffing, and services.

Further, private prison supporters' assertions that the private sector is more cost-efficient are largely unfounded. Whereas private prisons do demonstrate some cost savings, these savings are a result of lower salaries and benefits for nonunion employees and equally substandard food service and medical care for inmates. Similarly, the allegation that governments themselves can benefit financially by selling correctional facilities to private companies and through private-public initiatives for new facility construction are, also, largely illusory.[77] In fact, both a 1996 Government Accountability Office (GAO) study, as well as a University of Utah meta-analysis in 2009, demonstrated no clear advantage of private prisons in terms of costs.[78] Utah concluded that there is no quality of service improvement in private prisons whatsoever. Those studies that have alleged clear cost benefits by private prisons have been repeatedly disproven by nonpartisan organizations seeking the truth and not being spoon-fed political rhetoric many lawmakers seem to devour without a second thought.

In addition to private facilities' extreme cost-cutting in terms of personnel, which accounts for nearly two-thirds of a prison's operating budget, the second most expensive aspect of incarceration—programs—is also shortchanged. Thus, in addition to safety and security concerns from an undertrained, underpaid, and underperforming labor pool, programs which are critical for rehabilitation are also drastically cut, leaving many inmates who desire to better themselves discouraged with inadequate opportunities to do so. Education, vocational training, substance abuse treatment, anger management, and other mental health services are all critical aspects of successful rehabilitation, and private prisons have repeatedly shown that they fail miserably in all aspects.

Even more troubling, because the private sector is wholly profit driven, many questions arise as to private facilities' incentives to increase incarceration rates, lengthen sentences, foster high staff turnover rates, and contribute to high recidivism while simultaneously decreasing operating expenses. These interests are in direct opposition to the established goals of the criminal justice system in preventing crime and providing effective rehabilitation and deterrence toward lowering incarceration and recidivism rates. Accordingly, privatization undermines every crime control and punishment theory because a relentless push for profits overrides effective corrections and rehabilitation.

Accountability

Private prisons are overseen not by the government but by the private organizations that run them. Despite efforts by the ACA to enforce adherence to state laws as well as its own standards, it is quite easy for private facilities to falsify documents to promote the appearance of legitimacy and legality. ACA standards are touted as ensuring that private facilities comply with the legal atmosphere and provide high quality services when such is far from accurate. In fact, since public prisons are not required to adhere to said standards, privatization proponents claim that private facilities' requirement to comply with these standards automatically means that private facilities provide better quality services. Sadly, this is flawed logic and, overwhelmingly, not the case. The lack of direct supervision private prison administrators enjoy — particularly those in smaller, out-of-the-way "prison" towns—naturally fosters corruption and a cutting-corners mentality with the effects rippling through every aspect of the facility itself.

ACA accreditation standards are considered to be met if a facility can demonstrate a low number of inmate disturbances, few aggressive episodes, safe and relatively comfortable living environments, staff safety, and clear policies and procedures to ensure justice, order, safety, and security.[79] Accreditation is also supposed to examine the success of rehabilitative programs—education, vocational training, substance abuse treatment, and mental health services. As previously mentioned, it is extremely easy for facility administrators to report themselves in a positive light, regardless of the veracity of such claims. These facilities can reduce aggressive episodes and inmate disturbances by placing the facility on lockdown —

which, in New Mexico, happens quite frequently—so staff do not have to actually perform their duties.

In addition to giving the appearance of lower disturbances and aggressive episodes, frequent lockdowns also cause problems for ensuring that rehabilitative programs are effective because without participants there is no measure of success. In reality, accreditation simply relies on fabricated evidence of quality because the manner in which audits are conducted—not to mention the fact that prisons pay the ACA to conduct such audits—provides further incentive for granting accreditation in cases where it is not deserved.

Also worrisome is that many private prison companies provide substantial campaign contributions to legislators who push for increasing privatization opportunities. This is just another step toward rampant corruption. According to the Justice Policy Center, between 2003 and 2010, GEO Group donated over $1.5 million in state campaign contributions in Florida alone—where the company is headquartered—and also in states with legislation specifying a minimum number of inmate beds which must be maintained by private facilities.[80] Adding insult to injury is the growing number of class-action lawsuits several states such as Texas, New Mexico, and Ohio have filed demonstrating the increased risk to inmates from underqualified and poorly trained employees, as well as a pervasive system of corrupt judges who sentence offenders to private facilities in exchange for financial kickbacks.[81]

Finally, and perhaps most egregious, is that private prison companies in New Mexico are being run not by private correctional companies but, instead, by "real estate investment trusts."[82] Thus, instead of prisoners, inmates are classified as renters in the eyes of the federal tax system. Both CCA and GEO Group applied for and received Internal Revenue Service classification of their facilities as real estate investment trusts in order to save millions of dollars in taxes, lower capital costs, broaden shareholder benefits, increase flexibility for future growth opportunities, and improve business—not corrections—efficiency.[83] Not only is this wholly unethical but the primary reason for trusts' tax exemption status is that their only business function is to own real estate which is not the case with CCA and GEO Group. Running a prison is not the same as owning real estate and this blatant fraud has yet to be adequately addressed.

Privatization opponents assert that if legislators truly wish to address the widespread prison problem they should focus on sentencing reforms, diverting lower-level and nonviolent offenders into community corrections, correcting unfair sentencing disparities, promoting rehabilitation, and releasing inmates who no longer pose a danger to society such as the chronically ill or elderly. Simply increasing the number and use of private prisons fails at every level to promote the desired goals of the criminal justice system and, actually, does substantially more harm than good.

Reducing Private Prisons: An Emerging Trend

The federal government appears to understand the immense burden privatization places on the criminal justice system. In 2013, the DOJ identified several reforms touted as ensuring better allocation of federal resources and promoting more proportional solutions when it launched its Smart on Crime Initiative that has demonstrated declining federal prison populations. In fact, as of 2016, the DOJ housed 195,000 inmates in private facilities—down from a 2013 high of 220,000.[84] The cost savings are being reallocated to improving rehabilitative services to improve inmates' successful reentry and reintegration efforts.

Providing the impetus for widespread closures are recurring troubling reports criticizing private facilities' conditions. One in particular—the May 2012 death of a correctional officer during a riot at the CCA-run Adams County Correctional Center in Natchez, Mississippi—demonstrates how private prisons sacrifice safety, security, and inmate rehabilitation all in the name of the mighty dollar.[85]

Federal facilities are not the only ones facing closure. *The Denver Post* recently reported that the

CCA-run Kit Carson Correctional Center in Burlington, Colorado will become the sixth prison closed in the state over the past decade. Governor John Hickenlooper's office is now forced to mitigate the economic impact of the closure seeing as how the prison was Burlington's largest employer. Interestingly, however, this occurred after lawmakers paid a $9 million bailout to CCA in 2012 in order to keep the facility open.[86] To blame for the closure was the decreasing number of Colorado and out-of-state inmates, spearheaded by Idaho that recently pulled its state inmates from the facility. Because of CCA's contractual guarantee of a minimum number of inmates and demands for a higher daily rate per inmate than the state was willing to pay, the facility will be closing, with many other states in line to do the same.[87]

In New Mexico, merely one day after Deputy Attorney General Sally Yates' announcement that the DOJ would be reducing its private prison population, the state issued its plans to close the Cibola County Correctional Center near Grants. Run by CCA, the New Mexico Department of Corrections failed to issue a public reason for its decision. Following this announcement, both CCA and GEO Group witnessed a drop in shares by fifty and forty percent, respectively.[88]

In Texas, five private federal facilities are facing closure by the DOJ based on the aforementioned rising and indisputable evidence that private facilities do not save costs, fail to provide adequate safety and security, and are sorely inadequate with respect to educational and vocational programs to reduce recidivism. In fact, Yates has instructed the BOP to end or "substantially reduce" private contracts as they near renewal, and inmates would subsequently be transferred to BOP facilities.[89] In fact, the DOJ directive delineated its plan to reduce the total private federal prison population by fifty percent—to fewer than 14,200 inmates—by May 2017, and the federal government's own prisons have the space to accommodate the transfers since there has been a decrease in the overall federal prison population.[90] Thus, it appears that common sense is resurfacing. After all, with prisons' fundamental purpose being rehabilitating, privatization naturally places private facilities' economic motivations in direct conflict with their societal missions.[91]

Conclusion

The number of private prisons continues to swell at an exponential rate as evidenced by many states reporting their highest expenditures within the corrections sphere. Over the past fifteen years, corrections spending increased an incredible three hundred and fifty percent, compared to a two hundred and fifty percent growth rate for public welfare and a paltry one hundred and forty percent growth rate for education.[92] Of course, industry leaders such as CCA and GEO Group profit from this increase; so much, in fact, that CCA has been constructing prisons "on spec" absent any contracts or available prisoners to transfer to the new facilities.[93]

An oft-repeating theme is whether privatization serves the criminal justice system and upholds the fundamental tenets of criminal punishment and corrections or whether it is simply an economic boon for the private sector. Whereas some specifics of privatization may reduce certain costs, the pressing question is whether relinquishing corrections responsibility is legitimate or proper. Granted, government-run prisons have their share of problems such as rising gang violence, declining housing conditions, and chronic overcrowding. On the other hand, private facilities have their own share of endemic problems such as inexperienced and inadequate staff, higher contraband rates, more escapes, and building deficiencies thanks to the overuse of substandard materials in order to maximize profit.[94]

The line of demarcation between public and private institutions is not as clear as many would believe because some aspects of public prisons have and will always be private such as food service, medical care, and land use, for example. The only way to achieve a fully public system is within a totalitarian society, and the United States has not, as of yet, reached that state.[95] Prison privatization eschews the necessity for objective governmental actors to address and correct deviant behavior, and privatizing such an important function questions the credibility, efficacy, and legitimacy of the entire criminal justice system and raises serious questions as to whether crime prevention and deterrence are, in fact, a high priority.

Whichever side one advocates, the fact remains that the corrections system is not working. Increasing recidivism rates demonstrate without a doubt that current policies fail to correct behavior to facilitate reintegration and reentry for the tens of thousands of inmates released each month across the country. Coupled with numerous and often incompatible theories of punishment, the end result is that the American system is a disjointed mess that operates simply to maintain the status quo.

This is not to say that all privatization efforts are complete failures. Florida's Prison Rehabilitative Industries and Diversified Enterprises, Inc. (PRIDE) program has demonstrated considerable success in promoting significant rehabilitation by fostering meaningful work opportunities for inmates, instilling a necessary work ethic for post-release success, and simultaneously alleviating some victims' financial burdens.[96] Sadly, Florida's example is in the minority of privatization efforts.

In most cases, privatizing prisons does not address the problems at hand. It undermines every single crime control and punishment theory. Because private facilities seek to maximize their profits, providing effective rehabilitative programs, ensuring decent food and medical care for inmates, and maintaining a well-compensated and trained staff would challenge this goal. Government agencies appear to be listening. The BOP has joined the growing consensus that privately operated facilities have a greater turnover rate, more escapes, and utilize more staff than public state or federal prisons and, as such, should be drastically reduced and, ultimately, eradicated.

As previously mentioned, privatizing prisons neither ensures consistency nor protect inmates pursuant to the equal protection clause of the Fourteenth Amendment. Consequently, trust is eroded along with the ethical legitimacy of the criminal justice system itself because contracting out an important governmental function to the lowest bidder essentially negates the government's commitment to law and social accountability.

If the corrections system is to be fixed then legislators need to focus greater attention on the growing prison problem via sentencing reforms, diversion of nonviolent offenders into community corrections, a renewed commitment to rehabilitation, correcting unfair sentencing disparities, and releasing those inmates who do not pose a danger to society. Diversionary efforts such as specialized drug, domestic violence, and mental health courts have, in fact, demonstrated empirically valid improvements in rehabilitating offenders, saving money, and addressing the chronic overcrowding problem. Harsh and punitive penalties administered by those whose desire for profit overrides everything else does considerably more harm than good.

Natalie Faulk

Privatization is not the answer to the ongoing problems with the criminal justice system. Focusing attention and resources on addressing the root causes of crime and providing viable rehabilitative and educational programs—particularly in high-crime, predominantly minority communities where a disproportionate number of residents are incarcerated, thus leaving behind single mother families with fatherless children—will go further in alleviating the problem than the current path of increasing punishment, rising prison populations, chronic overcrowding, incessant construction of new private prisons, and high recidivism rates. Increasing, or even maintaining, the use of private prisons fails on every single level to achieve the criminal justice system's purpose and goals.

Mandatory Minimum Sentencing

Background

The fundamental principle of mandatory minimum sentencing requires that an individual who commits a particular crime be sentenced to a binding minimum prison term of a fixed and specific length. The explosive growth of mandatory minimum sentences is a result of the United States' high crime rates during the 1980's. Unfortunately, these sentences are grossly inflexible because they punish the offense specifically over the offender and virtually eliminate judges' abilities to fit a punishment to a crime. Interestingly, the issue of judicial discretion in sentencing provided the impetus for the advent of mandatory minimum sentencing.

A common theme throughout this book is the United States' ridiculously high incarceration rates. By the end of 2012, the United States had over 2.2 million people in prison.[97] Of particular concern is that despite the United States housing only five percent of the world's population, it imprisons twenty-five percent of the world's prisoners, and far more than countries with significantly larger populations.

Currently, there are over one hundred and seventy federal crimes on the books that carry mandatory minimum sentences, and this figure represents a seventy-eight percent increase since 1991.[98] Compounding the problem is that states have amassed their own list of offenses eligible for mandatory minimum sentences as well. The subsequent incarceration-happy policies of the American criminal justice system have severely undermined its effectiveness, failed to deter offenders, and contributed to increased recidivism — all while violating a number of ethical tenets — and requires serious overhaul.

Natalie Faulk

Problems Inherent to Mandatory Minimum Sentencing

There are five fundamental reasons why mandatory minimum sentencing practices should be changed: improve public safety, maintain realistic costs, reduce the drain on the criminal justice system and its limited resources, promote sentencing fairness, and uphold public desire. The first reason is public safety. Currently, nearly half of all federal prisoners are serving time for nonviolent drug offenses. Because of mandatory minimum sentences, more people are being incarcerated who would be better off in a diversionary program, and these individuals are getting locked up for longer periods of time. An emerging body of literature demonstrates that long mandatory minimum sentences fail to deter crime, yet policymakers and corrections officials continue to beat a dead horse, thinking that something will change. To paraphrase Albert Einstein, doing the same thing and expecting different results is the definition of insanity.

Second, the sheer cost of maintaining these sentences is enormous. According to Families against

Minimum Sentencing (FAMM), states have increased correctional spending by more than three hundred percent over the past two decades with taxpayers paying over $60 billion on incarceration each year, and this figure continues to rise.[99] If these exorbitant funds would have demonstrated improved deterrence and reduced recidivism then, perhaps, some support for mandatory minimums might be salvaged; however, in reality, increasingly longer sentences only augment costs and exert an overwhelming drain on the criminal justice system's rapidly decreasing resources which could be better utilized elsewhere than incarcerating nonviolent, low-level offenders.

This leads to the third reason: the immense drain on criminal justice resources. In order to address the growing costs of corrections with limited resources, spending in other areas such as crime fighting, equipment, probation and parole, community programs, and non-correctional staffing must be reduced. According to the DOJ, nearly twenty-five percent of its departmental funding is spent on incarcerating nonviolent offenders in federal prisons. Compounding the problem is that under mandatory minimum schemes, offenders are usually classified as a higher risk and sent to more secure facilities with greater costs and fewer rehabilitative programs.[100]

The next problem with mandatory minimum sentencing is due to its lack of fair practices. There is little debate that mandatory minimum sentencing practices are racially disparate. For example, the crack cocaine epidemic of the 1980's resulted in a push for mandatory minimum sentences for possession of crack. Because crack use is predominant among the Black population, the resulting laws resulted in large numbers of young Black people—largely males—being incarcerated for a ridiculously long time for a nonviolent drug offense when their White counterparts received less stringent sentences for possessing a larger quantity of powder cocaine.

Such arbitrary, harsh, and capricious policies evolved from outcry over widely disparate sentences handed out by judges as well as a desire to promote sentencing uniformity; however, in reality, they have simply exacerbated the issue by increasing criminogenic potential in some offender groups by institutionalizing them, reinforcing criminal behavior, and, essentially socializing them into an outsider subculture.[101] And throughout this, recidivism rises and the United States' incarceration rate continues to spiral out of control.

Sentence Reform Efforts

Providing insight into the abject failure of mandatory minimum sentences is Durkheim's collective conscience theory (1893). According to Durkheim, a society's collective conscience is a type of shared morality—or group think—which seeks to promote societal norms, values, and beliefs as to how society should operate, as well as to provide solutions for handling those who fail to abide by the collective laws.[102] Under this view, crime results from the failure of individuals to adhere to mainstream society's code and, in order to maintain order, criminal punishment is used to promote social solidarity by reaffirming said values and enforcing society's rules.[103] Despite making logical sense, an overly narrow focus fails to consider whether criminal punishments are effective. Mandatory minimum sentencing policies fail to promote Durkheim principles of social solidarity because of their inherent divisiveness and non-utility and their role in increasing the rift between the people and the criminal justice system because intended goals are not realized.

There has been some shift in public opinion regarding mandatory minimum sentencing as evidenced by polls demonstrating that as many as sixty percent of Americans oppose these sentencing practices for nonviolent offenders.[104] Additionally, respondents are overwhelmingly in favor of diverting money currently used to enforce such policies toward strengthening education, diversion, and community corrections programs. This issue is particularly salient in an unstable economy where funding is increasingly limited.

Some states have sought to reform their own mandatory minimum laws and have enjoyed success. In November 2013, California voters passed Proposition 36 that was geared toward reforming the state's "three strikes and you're out" law by changing the requirements for a third strike from any crime—whether violent or petty—to only a serious or violent felony. Voters realized that life sentences given to nonviolent offenders who did not truly pose a significant threat to public safety were an enormous waste of precious money that could be redirected elsewhere, not to mention that the offender himself or herself would be subject to more harm than good. By reforming the law and retroactively reducing nearly thirty-five hundred life sentences for offenders who were convicted of a third non-serious or nonviolent crime, California projected significant savings of as much as $100 million annually.[105]

The Downfall of American Corrections

Of course, for every success there is at least one failure. One example of a severely flawed mandatory minimum scheme is Oregon's Measure 11 (M11). Passed in 1994, this measure imposed long mandatory prison sentences ranging from seventy to three hundred months for sixteen designated violent and sex-related crimes, called for mandatory waivers of juveniles to adult court, and prohibited good time sentence reductions.[106] These policies were a result of concerns over the discrimination and disparity of indeterminate sentencing practices and judicial discretion; however, after the measure passed, several ethical concerns were raised—particularly with respect to mandatory waivers for juvenile offenders and the elimination of good time sentence reductions—and many realized that M11 was not the panacea for which they had hoped.

One of the greatest concerns was that even amidst mandatory minimum policies, the prosecutor has the greatest discretion and authority in determining whether a criminal defendant will be charged under the new laws or whether a plea bargain for a lesser offense is warranted to avoid implementation of a mandatory minimum sentence. Thus, the arbitrariness and sentencing disparity initially attributed to judges was simply subsumed by prosecutors and the myriad preexisting problems remained.

Merritt, Fain, and Turner (2006) conducted a study to determine how M11 was implemented, its effect on trial rates, any relevant characteristics shared by those who were sentenced pursuant to the new law, and its effect on the state's overall prison population. With data collected from the Oregon Department of Corrections and Oregon Criminal Justice Commission for the period 1993 through 1998, researchers examined sentencing trends following implementation of M11 expecting to find the law created a significant and substantial impact on the criminal justice system by increasing incarceration rates, particularly for minority offenders.

Their study demonstrated that prior to M11, sixty-six percent of eligible offenders were incarcerated and after implementation the rate increased to ninety percent. Additionally, the number of M11-alternate cases—those cases over which the prosecution exercised its discretion in how to charge offenders—nearly doubled during this same time frame. Thus, even with plea bargains in place to reduce M11-eligible offenses to M11-alternate offenses, a prison sentence remained the norm.[107]

Another finding was that before the initiative was enacted, M11-alternate offenders with no prior criminal history were usually sentenced to probation; however, after M11 was enacted, similarly situated offenders were sent to prison thirty percent of the time.[108] The data also demonstrated that not only were more offenders sentenced to prison, sentence length increased as well. Finally, the data suggested that the disproportionate representation of minorities remained the same. Thus, M11 failed to address preexisting concerns and simply transferred the right of indiscriminate discretion from judges to prosecutors.

Oregon's experience is not singular. Other jurisdictions that passed tougher sentencing legislation during the same time opened a Pandora's Box of unintended consequences and virtually no alleviation of discrimination directed against minorities and juveniles. Thus, whereas sentencing reform is necessary, it is equally necessary to consider the potential limitations of such reforms. Mandatory minimum sentencing failed to address the complexities of the situations in which such procedures were applied, and the criminal justice system continues to seek solutions for the same problems.

Conclusion

It should be clear that the motivation and ultimate goal of any punishment system is to prevent crime and reduce recidivism. Among the most popular efforts is incarceration; however, the evidence demonstrates rather convincingly that such efforts have failed. Modern punishment is predicated on the perceived ability to determine dangerousness in order to incapacitate offenders for an appropriate period of time to obtain the desired results. Whereas determinate sentences were created to make the criminal justice system more uniform in meting out punishment, the current approach fails to take into consideration mitigating and aggravating factors which are likely to call for different approaches. If the goal is to prevent reoffending then taking into account these differences and abandoning a failed one-size-fits-all system is critical.

One of the most glaring problems with current crime control policy and theory is the inherent dysfunction among certain elements. More specifically, rehabilitation is drastically different than incapacitation, deterrence, or retribution in that while the former seeks to help offenders, the latter three seek to harm them.[109] Compounding the problem are policies such as plea bargaining which further undermine punishment and sentencing by failing to ensure the uniformity mandatory minimum sentencing sought to achieve. Thus, offenders who take plea agreements often serve less time than their counterparts who decide to exercise their constitutional rights and proceed with a trial for the exact same offense.

Natalie Faulk

Retribution versus Rehabilitation

The Downfall of American Corrections

In its most basic application, a criminal justice system is necessary to impose deserved punishment, control potentially dangerous individuals, deter future crimes, and rehabilitate offenders in need.[110] As previously mentioned, punishment in the American criminal justice encompasses five fundamental goals: retribution, deterrence, incapacitation, rehabilitation, and, in some cases, restitution. Throughout the years, support for each goal has waxed and waned depending on a number of factors such as crime rates and the public's perception regarding offenders' potential dangerousness.

Retribution—or just deserts—addresses the offender's blameworthiness and is steeped in the biblical law of *lex talionis*, or "an eye for an eye, a tooth for a tooth." Retributive theory holds that an offender deserves punishment because of some social or moral transgression. Whereas this sounds like revenge, the primary difference is that revenge encompasses punishment sought to satisfy a singular victim while retribution is more concerned with punishing an offender for his or her immediate actions in order to protect society. Additionally, whereas revenge has no prescribed limits, retribution must adhere to policy.

There are several core principles on which effective punishments systems are based:

proportionality, consistency, transparency, and rationality. First, proportionality holds that a punishment should fit the crime for which it was prescribed while also considering the offender's criminal history. Logic dictates that the seriousness of the offense and the offender's criminal record should result in a longer sentence than the first-time offender who committed a nonviolent, relatively minor crime. Consistency—the second principle—is rather self-explanatory and stresses that similarly situated offenders should be punished similarly.

Finally, transparency and rationality are closely related. They both strive to mete out punishment according to specific rules while ensuring equal application of the law to all offenders as well as enabling others to examine said practices to ensure that what is prescribed is actually being done. Rationally, proper sentences should be the least restrictive to bring about the desired result whereas transparency forces sentencing judges to explain their rationale for a particular sentence. Of course, what should happen, more often than not, is not what actually does occur.

A serious problem with retributive punishment is proportionality. The advent of mandatory minimum sentencing—as previously discussed—assigns a set sanction for a particular crime without taking into consideration the individual offender. As a result, the potential for unfairness is heightened, essentially calling into question the criminal justice system's credibility as a whole. Another condemnation of retribution as a punishment is that it fails to attempt to change offenders' behavior, opting, instead, to castigate the individual for his or her actions.

Over the years there have been several proposed guidelines to address criminal sentencing that take into consideration the seriousness of the crime and offenders' criminal histories in devising appropriate punishments. Early guidelines were established to address widespread concern regarding judicial discretion and the lack of uniformity and equality when sentencing similarly situated offenders.[111] From this concern evolved truth in sentencing policies designed to promote predictability; however, as previously mentioned, the rising trend of mandatory minimum sentencing policies exacerbates the lack of uniformity and equality while wasting resources and contributing heavily to the overcrowding—and, subsequently, recidivism—problem.

With time, incapacitation became the cornerstone of American punishment and has resulted in the United States bearing the burdens of having the highest prison population in the world. In fact, not only does the United States have the highest imprisonment rate—incarcerating nearly ten times the number of inmates in other Western countries—but it also has the dubious distinction of being the only Western country that continues to use capital punishment. This underscores how a narrow focus on retribution and incapacitation as primary goals of criminal punishment damage a system, particularly with considerable evidence demonstrating the abject failure of this ideology.

How did the United States reach this point? During the 1970's, the United States' incarceration rate was quite similar to other Western industrialized nations. Also during that time, experimentation with alternative sentencing, victim-offender reconciliation, community service, and community-based corrections was prolific. The mindset at the time was that harsh and punitive punishments served little useful purpose and were not aligned with prevailing cultural norms.[112] Thus, individualized and indeterminate—and humane—sentencing policies that provided broad discretion to criminal justice system actors to customize punishments based on an offender's specific circumstances and needs characterized this era.

However, rising crime rates and increasing criticisms about the effectiveness of rehabilitation caused a shift from rehabilitation toward more retributive, punitive, determinate, and presumably uniform sentencing practices. Mandatory minimum sentencing was born to impart greater fairness and impartiality while early release and parole programs were discontinued. At the heart of this shift is a collective mentality that has responded to rising crime rates not by seeking to identify and address the root causes of crime but, instead, to impose increasingly harsher retributive punishment on offenders and, thus, exacerbate the problem.

Perhaps the greatest concern with this evolution is the overwhelming acceptance of retributive theory as a panacea for decreasing crime. Retribution requires that punishment be commensurate with an offender's blameworthiness or culpability; however, the advent of increasingly harsher sentences demonstrates certain punishments are not proportional to the crime committed. As previously mentioned, one of the most blatant examples is the crack cocaine mandatory minimum sentencing that unfairly punished certain—largely minority—offenders more harshly than other, non-minority ones.

Punishment is just only if it is "appropriately scaled between greater and lesser punishments accorded to more and less blameworthy offenders."[113] In other words, the totality of circumstances—not only with respect to the crime itself but also the offender's history—should guide an appropriate punishment. Unfortunately, modern retributive justice entails punishing an offender solely for his or her crime without any consideration of fairness and equality or mitigating and aggravating factors. Such blatant disregard can be seen in the increase in transferring juveniles to adult court, harsher probation and parole restrictions resulting in more revocations, a push for more zero tolerance policies, stricter sentence enhancements for certain aggravating circumstances, and enhanced sex offender surveillance. Granted, while many of these measures are, indeed, necessary to ensure public safety, said efforts have contributed to America's growing "addiction to punishment."[114]

Compounding the problem is a public that has been largely misinformed about crime as demonstrated by polls indicating widespread support for increasing punitive sanctions. Of primary concern is the public's belief that crime is increasing when, in fact, the evidence demonstrates crime has been steadily decreasing for years. The public is also largely unaware of statutory minimum sentences and sentencing alternatives such as diversionary courts and community-based corrections which have demonstrated significant success with nonviolent, first-time offenders.

The public learns the most about crime and punishment from mainstream media, and such misinformation is worrisome because of the tendency for public input to influence penal policies. The purpose of criminal punishment does have specific goals in place; however, growing and unsustainable prison populations beg loudly for alternatives to this snowballing retributive and punitive path down which this nation is traveling. A return to more rehabilitative oriented practices is sorely needed.

When the costs of the criminal justice system are examined, the figures are staggering. Whereas society would undoubtedly benefit from a diversion of funds to other areas such as education, health care, and assisting the homeless, there continues to be reluctance to do so. Investing rapidly decreasing valuable resources into a broken corrections system has usurped every other, more legitimate use for these resources. Further, the increased reliance on punitive and retributive policies perpetuates a vicious cycle of harsher sentences, increased public attention, and tougher legislation. Case in point, many states' "three strikes" laws highlight this problem. For example, California's law formerly mandated that any third felony—regardless of whether it was violent or not—triggers a sentence of life. It is obvious that this—and other similar statutes—was the result of continued pressure on policymakers absent any rational thought as to the long-term effects on the state's correctional system and budget, not to mention those communities with higher than average incarceration rates. Not only does incarceration affect the individual, but it also affects families, communities, and society in general. Thankfully, California lawmakers appear to have seen the error of their ways and have modified the state's "three strikes" law so nonviolent and relatively minor offenses do not trigger a third strike and, subsequently, a disproportionate punishment.

In an effort to improve criminal sentencing and punishment, and to address the problems of increasingly punitive sentencing policy, the concept of restorative justice emerged over the past few decades. Restorative justice seeks to shift the focus away from offenders and punitive sentencing to repairing the harm they caused society by forcing them to take responsibility, embrace accountability, mend the harm via restitution, and make both the victim and society whole. Restorative justice has been particularly successful with juvenile offenders who are still rather malleable and more amenable to rehabilitative efforts.

Despite this attention on restorative justice, the current American practice of criminal sentencing demonstrates an ongoing commitment to retribution at the expense of other goals. As such, it is easy to see how the various punishment goals can be at odds with each other, and absent a clear consensus among social scientists and the judiciary, these variations have led to confusion and inadequate punishments as evidenced by the continued high recidivism rate in this country.

In order to address an increasingly punitive and retributive correctional system, it is necessary to adjust collective ethical norms into a more manageable system because the increasing prison population is not sustainable. Criminal punishment must blend theory and practice into more proportional punishments which contain elements of retribution, deterrence, rehabilitation, and restorative justice. Certainly, some offenders are not amenable to rehabilitation and this is to be expected. However, a large proportion of offenders are, indeed, aware they made a mistake and do not want to make it again. These are the offenders who ought to receive the brunt of efforts and resources toward rehabilitation.

Final Thoughts

The Downfall of American Corrections

There is little disagreement that the American criminal justice system—especially corrections—is broken with no immediate feasible plan for repair. Whereas many people believe the answer to crime is to incarcerate everyone who breaks a law and throw away the key, this is an overly simplistic view given the vast majority of incarcerated offenders will eventually be released back into society. Harsher laws and imprisoning more and more people is not the answer. Instead, legislators and policymakers ought to reexamine the problem through a different lens: a lens guided by common sense, humanity, and logic.

Sadly, however, these qualities have fallen out of favor within the legal sphere over the past several decades; instead, being replaced by an overly vindictive, arrogant, and flawed ideology. Acts are deemed criminal based on mainstream society's views, norms, values, and beliefs. As previously mentioned, an act is not inherently criminal—except for certain ones such as murder and rape that are affronts to natural law—unless the "powers that be" determine it to be.

Draconian drug laws are the prime example of this ideological shift. The criminal justice system is not guided by justice; this is a misnomer, an oxymoron. If it were then everyone would enjoy their constitutional right to due process and equal protection under the law. Sadly, because this is not the case, the problem continues to worsen. The government has increasingly legislated acts which, in and of themselves, are not inherently criminal. Consequently, lawmakers have waged war on citizens' private lives and intruded to the point that many relatively innocuous behaviors have been elevated to the level of criminal deviance.

All of these issues beg greater attention by federal and state governments to address the revolving door of corrections and steadily increasing prison populations. Lawmakers and criminal justice system actors must be willing to take an honest look at the problem and devise a solution that does not involve simply locking more people up. The War on Drugs is an utter failure—not unlike the disastrous experiment that was Prohibition—and the enormous funds being thrown in this direction can be better allocated toward drug treatment, education, and even decriminalization to a degree. Additionally, mandatory minimum sentencing and the increasingly punitive knee-jerk policies that increase both time and likelihood of incarceration—particularly for minorities—must also be reexamined under a critical lens. Finally, addressing the blatant racial and ethnic disparities in the United States' criminal justice system must be discussed.

The Downfall of American Corrections

Of primary concern are the escalating prison population and the failed "solution" of simply constructing more facilities. The privatization boon has demonstrated that federal and state governments cannot sustain the increasing costs associated with such a high level of incarceration; however, private prisons are not the answer. Ongoing concerns about safety, security, and rehabilitation have repeatedly confirmed the rampant problems inherent to private facilities, not to mention the immorality of commoditizing human beings for profit.

Policymakers and lawmakers must take an honest look at the current state of American corrections without letting popular sentiment and emotion obscure reality. Dealing with crime and criminals will always be a part of any modern society; however, worsening an already escalating problem is most certainly not the answer. Taking rational stock of available resources and determining their best use is the only way to escape this vicious cycle in which the United States has been bitterly embroiled for several decades. It is time to stop wasting money and manpower beating one's head against the wall with no foreseeable end in sight. Paraphrasing Einstein again, doing the same thing over and over and expecting a different result is the very definition of insanity. Those with the ability to make a difference must think out of the proverbial box because current so-called solutions are not solving anything. In fact, they are making matters worse.

Notes

[1] R. Wertheimer, 1998, Constraining condemning, *Ethics, 108*(3), 493; G. Bradley, 2003, Retribution: The central aim of punishment, *Harvard Journal of Law & Public Policy, 27*(1).

[2] C. Banks, 2004, *Criminal justice ethics: Theory and practice*, Thousand Oaks, CA, Sage.

[3] P. Robinson, 2011, The ongoing revolution in punishment theory: Doing justice as controlling crime, *Arizona State Law Journal, 42*(4).

[4] A. Alschuler, 2003, The changing purposes of criminal punishment: A retrospective on the past century and some thoughts about the next, *The University of Chicago Law Review, 70*(1).

[5] Robinson, supra.

[6] Ibid.

[7] Ibid.

[8] C. Orthmann, 2012, *Introduction to law enforcement and criminal justice* (10th ed.), Clifton Park, NY, Delmar.

[9] M. Mulch, 2009, Crime and punishment in private prisons, *National Lawyers Guild Review, 66*(2).

[10] R. Johnson, A. Dobrzanska, and S. Palla, 2006, The American prison in historical perspective: Race, gender, and adjustment, in J. Pollock (Ed.), *Prisons: Today and Tomorrow* (2nd ed.), Sudbury, MA, Jones and Bartlett.

[11] Ibid.

[12] Ibid., 36.

[13] United States Department of Justice (DOJ), 2001, *Strategic plan 2001-2006—Goal 6*.

[14] P. Wagner, and B. Rabuy, 2016, Mass incarceration: The whole pie 2016, *Prison Policy Initiative*.

[15] Ibid.

[16] Ibid.

[17] N. Ghandnoosh, 2015, Black lives matter: Eliminating racial inequity in the criminal justice system, *The Sentencing Project*.

[18] Ibid.

[19] Rubenstein, E., 2016, The color of crime, 2016 revised edition, *American Renaissance*.

[20] Ibid.

[21] Ibid.

[22] Ibid.

[23] Ibid.

[24] H. Mac Donald, 2016, The myth of Black Lives Matter, *The Wall Street Journal*, 9 July.

[25] Ibid.

[26] Ibid.

[27] Ghandnoosh, supra.

[28] Ibid.

[29] Women's Prison Association (WPA), 2009, Prison nursery programs a growing trend in women's prisons.

[30] J. Laughlin, B. Arrigo, R. Blevins, and C. Coston, 2008, Incarcerated mothers and child visitation: A law, social science, and policy perspective, *Criminal Justice Policy Review, 19*(2).

[31] Ibid.

[32] A. Bronstein, 2005, Incarceration as a failed policy, *Corrections Today, 67*(5).

[33] M. Brickner, 2011, Prisons for profit, incarceration for sale, *Human Rights, 38*(3).

[34] Ibid.

[35] D. Miller, 2010, The drain of public prison systems and the role of privatization: An analysis of state correctional systems, *ProQuest Discovery Guides*.

[36] C. Mason, 2012, Too good to be true: Private prisons in America, *The Sentencing Project*.

[37] Ibid.

[38] S. Yates, 2016, Phasing out our use of private prisons, *United States Department of Justice*.

[39] Mason, supra.

[40] S. Terrell, 2013, Private prison companies' tax status turn inmates into 'renters,' *The New Mexican*, 23 April.

[41] Ibid., 5.

[42] Mason, supra, 5.

[43] Ibid.

[44] B. Sarabi, and E. Bender, 2000, The prison payoff: The role of politics and private prisons in the incarceration boom, *Western Prison Project/Western States Center*.

[45] Ibid.

[46] T. Clear, G. Cole, and M. Reisig, 2011, *American corrections* (9th ed.), Belmont, CA, Wadsworth.

[47] Ibid.

[48] Mason, supra.

[49] Miller, supra.

[50] Mulch, supra.

[51] Miller, supra.

[52] Mason, supra.

[53] Miller, supra.

[54] Ibid.; Mulch, supra; Brickner, supra.

[55] Mason, supra, 14-15.

[56] Ibid.

[57] C. Smith, 2016, Why the U.S. is right to move away from private prisons, *The New Yorker*, 24 Aug.

[58] Ibid.

[59] Mulch, supra, 74.

[60] Miller, supra; D. Perrone, and T. Pratt, 2003, Comparing the quality of confinement and cost-effectiveness of public versus private prisons: What we know, why we do not know more, and where to go from here, *The Prison Journal, 83*(3).

[61] Brickner, supra.

[62] C. James, 2012, Prisons for profit in the United States: Retribution and means vs. ends, *Journal for Human Rights/Zeitschrift Fur Menschenrechte, 6*(1).

[63] Miller, supra.

[64] Brickner, supra.

[65] S. Lee, 2012, By the numbers: The U.S.'s growing for-profit detention industry, *ProPublica*.

[66] Mason, supra, 11.

[67] Ibid.

[68] "New Mexico slaps private prison companies with $1.4 million in fines," 2013, *Prison Legal News*.

[69] Ibid.

[70] Lee, supra.

[71] "New Mexico,"supra.

[72] L. Timar, 1990, Privatizing prisons (cover story), *IPA Review*, 44(1).

[73] Mulch, supra, 74.

[74] Brickner, supra.

[75] James, supra.

[76] Lee, supra.

[77] Mason, supra.

[78] Ibid.

[79] Miller, supra.

[80] Brickner, supra.

[81] J. Greene, 2000, Prison privatization: Recent developments in the United States, *Paper Presented at ICOPA, Toronto, Canada, 12 May 2000*.

[82] Terrell, supra.

[83] Ibid.

[84] Yates, supra.

[85] J. Sanburn, 2016, The U.S. is ending private prisons for federal inmates. So where will the prisoners go? *Time*, 18 August.

[86] J. Brown, and K. Mitchell, 2016, Kit Carson prison in Burlington to close; 142 jobs lost, *The Denver Post*, 22 July.

[87] Ibid.

[88] J. Cardillo, 2016, A look at the private prison industry's New Mexico presence, *Albuquerque Business First*, 19 Aug.

[89] D. Schiller, 2016, Closure of private prisons could hit Texas in pocketbook, *Houston Chronicle*, 5 Sept.

[90] Sanburn, supra.

[91] Smith, supra.

[92] Mulch, supra.

[93] Ibid.

[94] S. Camp, and G. Gaes, 2001, Growth and quality of U.S. private prisons: Evidence form a national survey, *Criminology & Public Policy*, 1(3).

[95] Mulch, supra.

[96] Timar, supra.

[97] R. Cassidy, 2013, (Ad)ministering justice: A prosecutor's ethical duty to support sentencing reform, *Boston College Law School Legal Studies Research Paper Series*.

[98] Ibid.

[99] Families against Mandatory Minimums (FAMM), 2013, Recent state-level reforms to mandatory minimum laws, 13 June.

[100] Cassidy, supra.

[101] Ibid.

[102] P. Smith, 2008, Durkheim and criminology: Reconstructing the legacy, *Australian & New Zealand Journal of Criminology*, 41(3).

[103] C. Banks, 2013, *Criminal justice Ethics: Theory and practice* (3rd ed.), Thousand Oaks, CA, Sage.

[104] FAMM, supra.

[105] Ibid.

[106] N. Merritt, T. Fain, and S. Turner, 2006, Oregon's get tough sentencing reform: A lesson in justice system adaptation, *Criminology & Public Policy*, 5(1).

[107] Ibid.

[108] Ibid.

[109] A. Price, and B. Stitt, 1986, Consistent crime control philosophy and policy: A theoretical analysis, *Criminal Justice Review*, 11(2).

[110] Robinson, supra.

[111] R. Lubitz, and T. Ross, 2001, Sentencing guidelines: Reflections on the future, *Sentencing & Corrections: Issues for the 21st Century*.

[112] M. Tonry, 2007, Looking back to see the future of punishment in America, *Social Research*, 74(2).

[113] Ibid.

[114] G. Bazemore, 2007, The expansion of punishment and the restriction of justice: Loss of limits in the implementation of retributive policy, *Social Research*, 74(2), 652.

Bibliography

Alschuler, A. (2003, Winter). The changing purposes of criminal punishment: A retrospective on the past century and some thoughts about the next. *The University of Chicago Law Review, 70*(1), 1-22.

Banks, C. (2004). *Criminal justice ethics: Theory and practice*. Thousand Oaks, CA: Sage.

Banks, C. (2013). *Criminal justice ethics: Theory and practice* (3rd ed.). Thousand Oaks, CA: Sage.

Bazemore, G. (2007, Summer). The expansion of punishment and the restriction of justice: Loss of limits in the implementation of retributive policy. *Social Research, 74*(2), 651-662.

Bradley, G. (2003, Fall). Retribution: The central aim of punishment. *Harvard Journal of Law & Public Policy, 27*(1), 19-31.

Brickner, M. (2011). Prisons for profit, incarceration for sale. *Human Rights, 38*(3), 14.

Bronstein, A. (2005, Aug.). Incarceration as a failed policy. *Corrections Today, 67*(5), 6-13.

Brown, J., & Mitchell, K. (2016, 22 July). Kit Carson prison in Burlington to close; 142 jobs lost. *The Denver Post.*

Camp, S., & Gaes, G. (2002). Growth and quality of U.S. private prisons: Evidence from a national survey. *Criminology & Public Policy, 1*(3), 1-18.

Cardillo, J. (2016, 19 Aug.). A look at the private prison industry's New Mexico presence. *Albuquerque Business First.*

Cassidy, R. (2013, 19 Sept.). (Ad)ministering justice: A prosecutor's ethical duty to support sentencing reform. *Boston College Law School Legal Studies Research Paper Series, 314.*

Clear, T., Cole, G., & Reisig, M. (2011). *American corrections* (9th ed.). Belmont, CA: Wadsworth.

Families against Mandatory Minimums (FAMM). (2013, 13 June). Recent state-level reforms to mandatory minimum laws.

Ghandnoosh, N. (2015, 3 Feb.). Black lives matter: Eliminating racial inequity in the criminal justice system. *The Sentencing Project*, 1-27.

Greene, J. (2000). Prison privatization: Recent developments in the United States. *Paper Presented at ICOPA, Toronto, Canada, 12 May 2000.*

James, C. (2012). Prisons for profit in the United States: Retribution and means vs. ends. *Journal for Human Rights/Zeitschrift Fur Menschenrechte, 6*(1), 76-93.

Johnson, R., Dobrzanska, A., & Palla, S. (2006). The American prison in historical perspective: Race, gender, and adjustment. In J. Pollock (Ed.). *Prisons: Today and Tomorrow* (2nd ed.). Sudbury, MA: Jones and Bartlett.

Laughlin, J., Arrigo, B., Blevins, R., and Coston, C. (2008, June). Incarcerated mothers and child visitation: A law, social science, and policy perspective. *Criminal Justice Policy Review, 19*(2), 215-238.

Lee, S. (2012, 20 June). By the numbers: The U.S.'s growing for-profit detention industry. *ProPublica.*

Lubitz, R., & Ross, T. (2001, June). Sentencing guidelines: Reflections on the future. *Sentencing & Corrections: Issues for the 21st Century, 10.*

Mac Donald, H. (2016, 9 July). The myth of Black Lives Matter. *The Wall Street Journal.*

Mason, C. (2012, Jan.). Too good to be true: Private prisons in America. *The Sentencing Project.*

Merritt, N., Fain, T., & Turner, S. (2006, Feb.). Oregon's get tough sentencing reform: A lesson in justice system adaptation. *Criminology & Public Policy, 5*(1), 5-36.

Miller, D. (2010, Feb.). The drain of public prison systems and the role of privatization: An analysis of state correctional systems. *ProQuest Discovery Guides.*

Mulch, M. (2009). Crime and punishment in private prisons. *National Lawyers Guild Review, 66*(2), 70-94.

New Mexico slaps private prison companies with $1.4 million in fines. (2013, Jan.). *Prison Legal News,* 40.

Orthmann, C. (2012). *Introduction to law enforcement and criminal justice* (10th ed.). Clifton Park, NY: Delmar.

Perrone, D., & Pratt, T. (2003). Comparing the quality of confinement and cost-effectiveness of public versus private prisons: What we know, why we do not know more, and where to go from here. *The Prison Journal, 83*(3), 301-322.

Price, A., & Stitt, B. (1986). Consistent crime control philosophy and policy: A theoretical analysis. *Criminal Justice Review, 11*(2), 23-30.

Robinson, P. (2011). The ongoing revolution in punishment theory: Doing justice as controlling crime. *Arizona State Law Journal, 42*(4), 1089-1111.

Rubenstein, E. (2016). The color of crime, 2016 revised edition. *American Renaissance.*

Sanburn, J. (2016, 18 Aug.). The U.S. is ending private prisons for federal inmates. So where will the prisoners go? *Time.*

Sarabi, B., & Bender, E. (2000, Nov.). The prison payoff: The role of politics and private prisons in the incarceration boom. *Western Prison Project/Western States Center.*

Schiller, D. (2016, 5 Sept.). Closure of private prisons could hit Texas in pocketbook. *Houston Chronicle.*

Smith, C. (2016, 24 Aug.). Why the U.S. is right to move away from private prisons. *The New Yorker.*

Smith, P, (2008). Durkheim and criminology: Reconstructing the legacy. *Australian & New Zealand Journal of Criminology, 41*(3), 333-344.

Terrell, S. (2013, 23 April). Private prison companies' tax status turn inmates into 'renters.' *The New Mexican.*

Timar, L. (1990). Privatizing prisons. (Cover story). *IPA Review, 44*(1), 41.

Tonry, M. (2007, Summer). Looking back to see the future of punishment in America. *Social Research, 74*(2), 353-378.

United States Department of Justice (DOJ). (2001). Strategic plan 2001-2006– Goal 6.

Wagner, P., & Rabuy, B. (2016, 14 Mar.). Mass incarceration: The whole pie 2016. *Prison Policy Initiative.*

Wertheimer, R. (1998, Apr.). Constraining condemning. *Ethics,108*(3), 489-501.

Women's Prison Association (WPA). (2009, 13 July). Prison nursery programs a growing trend in women's prisons.

Yates, S. (2016, 18 Aug.). Phasing out our use of private prisons. *United States Department of Justice.*